I ♥ ME
FEATURING THE "MY BAD" BUNCH!
AUTHOR:
ANDREA BIERRIA
MS. Sped & Ed, life coach & yoga instructor. Inspiring Actress
BLACK PRIDE
AF440925

I  Me

featuring the "my bad" bunch!

By

Andrea Bierria

MS.Sped & Ms.Ed, life coach & yoga instructor. Aspiring Actress.

Author's Liberty Agency
244 5th Ave New York NY 10001

Website: www.authorsliberty.com
Hotline: 1-(646)844-9622
Email: info@authorsliberty.com

Ordering Information:
Quantity sales. Special discounts are available on quantity purchases by corporations, associations, and others. For details, contact the publisher at the address above.

I  Me

featuring the "my bad" bunch!

Table of Contents

<u>*FOREWORD*</u>

The purpose of this book is to help build your confidence. To help build a clear purpose for your life. This book is dedicated to all future middle schoolers who are seeking guidance on how to tackle this big gigantic confusing world. First and foremost, always seek advice from a responsible adult such as it be your parents, grandparents, or other guardians in your life a god parent or a favorite aunt or uncle, or even your favorite teacher. And never keep secrets from your parents or guardians keeping secrets means you have something to hide and your too young to hide things. There is no situation that you have encountered, that you cannot share with someone. If you are approached by anyone even someone you know, to keep a secret, talk, talk and talk to someone.

Our first activity is for you to pick out a name for yourself that explains one of your best attributes. My name is Andrea, so I choose to call myself amazing Andrea. The word amazing begins with the letter A and so does my name. The word amazing is how I feel about myself. My talents, my smile, my laugh, and my personality. Can you think of an acronym that begins with the first letter of your name? Let's say your name begins with A and you chose Amazing Abby, why are you amazing, I am amazing because I like to help people. I like to walk my dog, or I like to watch tv with my grandparents, whatever you feel makes you special. Remember, I love me means just that. I love me! For whatever reason you choose. Doing a good deed does make us feel special and helpful, but sometimes it's small things that makes a big deal. Like telling someone how much they mean to you, and saying the word thank you and please really gives you a badge of honor. Those words make you a hero! If you were in my yoga class, I would consider you a warrior! A warrior is a real nice person who is confident and stands firm in their beliefs. Now, Let us see your warrior stance!

Our next activity is to write a mission statement that creates goals and boundaries. I believe that I am great, I can do all things. That I am allowed to do left! I respect myself; I respect others, I respect who I am and who I strive to be.

My vision statement allows you to see yourself, even at your age you can see yourself as the best volleyball player or jump rope jumper.

My vision statement is I see myself climbing mountains. Breaking down barriers. Rising to the top my game. I see myself happy and living my best life! As you write your vision statement, think of something that you like to do. If you like playing basketball, dancing, rapping, or cooking, babysitting. Write down what you like to do and why? Practice makes perfect, so whatever your hobby is, perfect it means practice as much as you can to get better. Remember boys and girl's schoolwork comes first!

Now you should be able to write your mission statement and your vision statement in your journal. And remember to use your special name you picked for yourself, example, I Am amazing Andrea my mission is to….and I am amazing Andrea, I vision myself….

MISSION STATEMENT

Name:

Mission Statement:

Vision Statement:

What do I like about myself?

What makes me special?

What is my special hobby and why?

<h1 style="text-align:center">VISION BOARD</h1>

A Vision Board reminds us of our goals yes students your vision board is what you create to document what you are reaching towards. You are not expected to write your plans as a future doctor. Your goals are in your immediate future. Example: your vision board may include an obstacle you are facing that you would like to fix such as acing a math test, learning a different language etc. remember those are your goals and your goals only, you can however, talk with your parents about your vison board so they can help you achieve those goals and also monitor your progress.

Warriors make your goals attainable. This is a fun project, so warriors, have fun, and discuss something like learning to ride a bike or learning to swim with your parents, they must schedule this goal and make allowances. Remember your goals will be revisited to see how your coming along with this goal.

My vision board

My goals   **time frame**   **completion date**

WHAT AM I GOING TO BE WHEN I GROW UP?

featuring Jen and Lynn from the "My Bad" Bunch

By Andrea Bierria

BLACK
PRIDE

WHAT AM I GOING TO BE WHEN I GROW UP?

JEN: I don't Know what I want to be.

LYNN: For what? Halloween? I thought you were going as Jason.

JEN: No not for Halloween. Forever.

LYNN: Forever? Like a j o b?

JEN: More like a career. Like a nurse or a teacher.

LYNN: Wow, youre growing up too fast. Wow. I sound like my moms. Lets just stay as we are kids that rides skateboards and occasionally throw that garbage out for $5.

JEN: $5? Im really scared now. And besides, I only get $2.

LYNN: I know. Lets go to Ms. B She helps you decide what youd like to be?

JEN: That's right Isn't She the school nurse?

LYNN: Ah, yeah, thats her day job.

BLACK
PRIDE

TEACHER ANDREA: Hey, you too. Good to see you all. Now, grab a seat. Any questions? What do we do, class?

STUDENTS: Raise your hand and wait to be called.

TEACHER ANDREA: Right, class. Well, any questions?

JEN: Well, uh, how did you know you wanted to be a nurse?

TEACHER ANDREA: Well, I always liked helping people. And if the neighborhood dogs or cats got hurt, I would bandage them up.

JEN: So that's how you know.

TEACHER ANDREA: I need to explore a little information about yourselves.

LYNN: Oh, boy. It's work time.

JEN: Everyone will hear you.

LYNN: That's the whole idea. Yeah.

TEACHER ANDREA: Tell me, boys and girls, what do you like about yourselves?

JEN: I like my smile.

LYNN: I like my bike riding skills. I can do papa wheelies.

TEACHER ANDREA: What makes you special?

JEN: I am special. Hmmm. I have a lot of friends.

LYNN: My mom says I am special cause I look like my grandma.

TEACHER ANDREA: What is your special hobby and why?

JEN: I like to do yoga.

LYNN: She really does. I, on the other hand, like to help my mom cook and bake cakes. I even get to frost the cakes.

TEACHER ANDREA: Well thats great. Boys and girls, you have passed the test with flying colors. We have to love ourselves and appreciate what makes us special. Well all have a special talent, whether its big or small. If we keep practicing our special talents, we grow to love what we do and get better at it.

I LOVE ME GLOSSARY

I love me glossary, please pick three words that pertain to you. Write a sentence that begins with, I have or I am, you can pick your own words as well! Say these sentences each day! If you say each word in a sentence, you will build confidence in your self. so pick out your favorite word that best suits you. Look in the mirror as you read your strengthening sentence. I will start with my favorite sentence/phrase I believe in my self, I am great. I will achieve greatness.

Confident

Self esteem

Courageous

Creative

Assertiveness

Important

LET's MEDITATE

Okay Warriors lets meditate: *Please ask parents before you do any Yoga Practices.*

Having a bad day how about meditating, what are the benefits of meditation? To focus,

have clarity, reduce anxiety, and to regulate your emotions.

Relax close your eyes

Think of a flower that has pretty colors

As you look at the flower picture the flower growing

Or picture yourself smelling the flower

This is only done for about one- two- minutes

Birthday cake

Picture yourself at a birthday party your surrounded by your family and friends and

picture a birthday cake with candles, warriors take a deep breath and blow out the

candles and your done! Feel better? Well you have just set the reset button!

BLA
BLACK PRIDE
BLACK PRIDE

Warriors, what is your daily routine? Example, when I wake, I stretch my arms high towards the sky and I'm grateful for seeing another day! I brush my teeth and say hello to my family! And we eat breakfast. Halt warriors make your bed, if you have time and aren't not running late!

Sometimes warriors, if your days starts out strange or confusing, it's just for the moment it doesn't determine how your day will be. That is why it's important to get rest at night so you can have a positive morning. Why are we doing this? To start our day positively, organized and to build a routine. Thanking someone shows humility, stretching creates positive energy, and making your bed begins a routine of doing chores, which most of us do not allow our children do! Another thing you may do before you leave the house is to blow out the candles and smell the flowers. This will help us reduce stress, enhance awareness and focus your mind.

BLACK
PRIDE

QUALITIES OF A LEADER

What are qualities of a leader? Who is your favorite leader and why?

I like Martin Luther King, he is a peace warrior, he instilled peace in the world. He dedicated his life for "everyone" to have world peace. It is important to have a leader that you admire and a person of many quotes. Example: Maya Angelou is a person of many quotes and attributes, one of her famous quotes is: I know why the caged bird sings! Or Nothing will work unless you do!

If you were a leader what type of rules would you create?

How would you convey messages of leadership skills?

Can you make up your own quote? Warriors I invite you to have fun with this portion, of "I love me"

Be silly, make up rhymes, go for it! Your quote belongs to you! So be different, be original.

Why am I different?

Warriors it's ok to be different, let's say you come from another country, or from another school. Everyone wants to be liked and feel welcomed sometimes when you're the new kid on the block you might feel that you're not accepted by your peers, colleagues, neighbors, we can celebrate diversity by welcoming our new friends, bullying and teasing is played out, no one's doing that anymore. Most of us have diversified backgrounds, my father's side of the family comes from Cuba, New Orleans and my mothers' side of my family is Puerto Rican.

School integration-invite the students to talk about where he or she comes from!

School curriculum-draw a flag, talk about national dishes.

Community connection- invite newcomers to community meeting and outings and let's celebrate diversity together!

<u>WHY AM I ALWAYS SO ANGRY?</u>

Warriors, sometimes there are things going on beyond our control! It's not your Fault! Shake it off! Do not carry your situations/problems to school or take out your anger against anyone and if you do please apologize immediately! Do not let your problems deter you from becoming great! There are plenty of resources to help you deal and cope with your situation. What can you do to help diffuse your anger?

<u>*Suggestions:*</u>

<u>*Take a few minutes and just breathe in and out .*</u>

<u>*Possibly walk away from the anger point.*</u>

<u>*Talk with someone.*</u>

<u>*Hit the Reset button, do not hold on to anger.*</u>

BLACK
PRIDE

<u>FINAL MESSAGE</u>

Okay Warriors here is the final message of the I love me series 1st handbook

The "My Bad" bunch. The message here don't let anyone talk you into doing something

that you know is wrong Let's encourage each other to make good choices and its ok to

not follow a crowd if it means getting into trouble

<u>*Jenn:*</u> *Hi Lynn*

Tobias: Hey you two, want to cut class?

Jen: Well cutting is bad

Tobias: Ah come on, well be back in time for the bus!

Jenn: I can't I got into so much trouble, the last time, my mom was furious, and I had double chores and no phone, no thank you!

Lynn: I am down!

Tobias: Great! Let's go!

Jen: Bye (Jenn walks to class)

Lynn: Ok where we headed?

Tobias: We are going to meet up with Ely

Lynn: But Ely well ah, likes to steal.

Tobias: He never got caught, and it's not proven

Lynn: Well everyone thinks he is a thief and that is bad!

Tobias: Who cares what everybody thinks.

Lynn: Well what are we doing?

Tobias: We just chilling playing the games and whatever!

They meet up with Ely

Ely: Hey what's up welcome to the cut class house dweebs. Lol

Lynn: Hey what's up!

Tobias: You got food dude

Ely: No, this is not the cafeteria

Lynn: Thank Goodness!

Tobias: Well I am hungry let's walk to the store.

Lynn: Who has money

Ely: Not I said the poor guy

Tobias: Not I but I have an idea.

Tthey get to the store and huddle and talk about their plan.

Lynn walks in and distracts the manager /store clerk and ask about an item.

Ely and Tobias go in the store after Lynn and are circling around in different directions.

Lynn is still trying to distract the clerks.

However, the clerk gets suspicious and starts looking at the two boys,

Although they had nothing in their hands or pockets, they all start screaming go!

WALLY WORLD
BLACK PRIDE

The three make a dash for the door. As soon as they come outside, the police were in front of the store.

WALLY WORLD
Yeah I got em!

Although they hadn't taken anything from the store. Even though they were in the

Store during school hours and with out any money The "My bad" bunch gets banned

from the store unless they are accompenied by an adult! Or after School hours.

Their parents were disappointed and the bunch had to promise they would not do it

again. Oh and the parents informed the store manager that since their kids like going

to the store so much how about letting them throw out the garbage and sweep the

place for a week

<u>*Reflection:*</u>

Hello Warriors, I hope you enjoyed this book but mostly I hope you can refer to certain strategies like Coping with anger and ways to relieve Stress by meditating, talking and working things out when your feeling down. Building confidence in your self by saying your confirmations daily. Also being kind to your self and others and most importanly not following a crowd of mischef. Well bye for now warriors.

Ms. B

SCHOOL
STOP
BLACK PRIDE

Think of your actions and what the consequences would be!

The moral of the story is please watch the crowd your with. Lynn knew her friends were trouble and she went anyway.

The End!

<u>DEDICATION PAGE</u>

I dedicate this book to all the warriors of the Univers!

Stand Tall Warriors!

I dedicate this book to my children Brandon, Justin, my nephews Andre, Arin Bryson

and Nieces, Racine, Faythe and Ashley. And my mom Helen, Ms. Lester and Ms. Minatee and

all my besties! Barrios and Sanchez, Mrs. Walker, Mrs. Grant, Esperanza, The Bierria's

The Smith's The Walker Family, Marcelin, Collazo's, Reyes Family and Sanchez Family

My sis Denise, April, Dianne, Beanie, Niecey, Sue, Monique, Syeda, Jill, Caraissia,

Badria, Melody, Val, Bro Sha, Cesare, Quentin, Jimmy, Lusaka, Angie, Tori, Sandra,

Zenobia, Taleta, Olga, Jeannie, Stephanie, Gem, Precious, Felicia, Duck, Tawana, Camille,

TeeTee, Dyan, Elaine, Ronis, Renee, Natasha, Yvonne, Bird, Omari, Mr. Gold, Marvisa,

Alamay, Michelle, Tiffany, Luke, Andrea, Ms. Bennet, Mrs. Bashir, Mr. Howard, Chrissy,

Evelyn and The entire 45 Crew Dr. Jones and Ms. Guzman

To my step daughters Ajahnae, Santina Shelana and Gabriella

The love of my life my husband Charles Watson. And my stepdaughter, Gabriella Watson a future warrior! and the entire Watson Family, I love you all!

I also want to thank My prayer line Family, My Yoga Family! Sis Connie and Minister Desiree, You two are awesome! Rinnay, Vanessa,

All my places of work, Internships and Trainings, to David and Nan! My acting Coaches- Will Gilly Productions

Department of Education

Newburgh Enlarged School District

Breathe for Change, YMCA

Boys and Girls Club

Girl Scouts of America

Boys Scouts of America

Charlie William Chris

Brandon and Justin

Brother Curtis! Hit that reset button. Thank You.

Young & Unique Christian Daycare

Restore Your Power Tutoring Service

Walden Police Department

Law Offices of Sobo & Sobo

G and H Deli

Eddys Jerk Center

Rommel Millian Physical Therapy

Terrace Lounge

My Churches:

Andre Cook Ministries

Greater Love Deliverance Church

Walden Baptist Church

Mount Carmel Church of Christ

Tabernacle of Faith Christian Fellowship

Best Temple Church of God in Christ

Ebenezer Baptist Church

New Life Pentecostal Church

Next Level Living

The Morgan Family

Dedicated to all those who lost their lives due to Co Vid-19

In Memory to Crystal, J.C, Dotty, Miguel, Sam, Mildred, Ebony, Mrs. Virginia,

Stephanie, Karen, Grandma Isabel, Grandma Rose, Carlos Sanchez, Steve, Ms. Depass,

Norma, and Johnny, Tasha, Joelle, Leah, Chico, Meeka.

The Next Chapter Featuring the "My Bad " Bunch

By Andrea Bierria

I THINK I LIKE HER
feat.
Tobias, Elly and Coach Higgins

THE "MY BAD" BUNCH!

TOBIAS: Yo, Ely. Have you seen Jen?

ELY: Jen? Na, not today.

TOBIAS: No, dude. Have you seen Jen Ely? Like, looking at Jen like a hot chic?

ELY: Nope. Definitely not. Matter of fact, dude, here's the number to my Optum threat.

TOBIAS: It's optometrist and my vision is just fine.

ELY: How many fingers am I holding up?

TOBIAS: You're holding up a baseball mitt.

ELY: So you're seeing illusions?

COACH HIGGINS: Hey, boys ready to practice. Give me some laps.

ELY: Tobias can't do laps. He has a crush on somebody.

TOBIAS: I wouldn't go for that far, but I do think she's kind of cute.

COACH HIGGINS: Well, come on, boys. Nothing wrong with having a girlfriend. You know, someone to pal around with. I remember that's how me and my wife started over 40 years ago.

ELY: Oh, ok. Tobias. You're in big trouble. You only 39 more years to go.

TOBIAS: Ah, forget it. What's with you? Two? I went from a teenager with a crush to being an old married man.

COACH HIGGINS: Well, Son, Welcome to my world.

We are cordially invited to the 9th Grade Picture featuring the "My Bad" Bunch!

THE "MY BAD" BUNCH!

JEN: *I can't wait for the dance.*

LYNN: *Me either. You want a dress alike?*

JEN: *No way. Are you kidding me? This is a time uniqueness, not double trouble. Anyways, I'm going to make my own dress.*

LYNN: *Why are you going to do that? I'm going to order my dress from Fancy's.*

JEN: *Well, I'm going to look original.*

LYNN: *Yeah, an original hot mess. My bad. You wanna go buy some fake nails?*

JEN: *Sure. Let's go to Fancy's. They have a sale. Two for five bucks. So you need three. And I have three saved.*

JEN: *Hey, what are you guys doing here?*

TOBIAS: *Shopping for the dance?*

ELY: *Yeah, getting jiggy with it.*

JEN: *Nice moves, Ely. I see you've been practising.*

ELY: *Not really in a natural like Michael J.*

TOBIAS: *Well, it fancy seeing you here, Jen.*

JEN: *Well, we are at fancy's Get it?*

ELY: *Yeah Yeah, Fancy Snancy.*

LYNN: *Well, off we go dudes, we have some shopping to do.*

TOBIAS: *Call me Jen, save a dance for me,*

ELY: *Dude, why not ask her to the dance?*

TOBIAS: *What if she says no?*

ELY: *Of course she's gonna say no. When has that ever stopped you?*

TOBIAS: *Hey Jen, Do you want to uh, uh, go to the pet section I hear they have new hummingbirds.*

ELY: *Dude What? Hummingbirds?*

JEN: *Well I'd love to, but Lynn and I have other plans. But maybe later we'll meet you guys there.*

LYNN: *Why?*

ELY: *Good question.*

TOBIAS: *How about in two hours?*

ELY: *My curfew isn't until 8 p.m. tonight,*

JEN&LYNN: *Ok? See ya!*

Hey! what's up Tobias?

THE "MY BAD" BUNCH!

JEN: Hey what's up, Tobias?

TOBIAS: Hey Jen.

JEN: Sorry I missed you the other day.

TOBIAS: Well we waited a while while watching the new birds.

JEN: OK,ok, Fascinating.

TOBIAS: Do you want to go to the dance with with

JEN: With you Tobias?

TOBIAS: Yeah with me.

JEN: Well… can I think about it because….

TOBIAS: You were asked already!

JEN: Sort of By Lynn

TOBIAS: Lynn! Well, why don't you and Lynn join me and Ely?

JEN: Well that would be nice. I tell Lynn

TOBIAS: And I tell a Ely, and no matter what he says are going

THE END

www.ingramcontent.com/pod-product-compliance
Lightning Source LLC
Chambersburg PA
CBHW080809120726

48001CB00009B/2882